All That Glitters
A Kid's Guide To Virginia City, Nevada

Photography By John D. Weigand
Poetry By Penelope Dyan

Bellissima Publishing, LLC
Jamul, California
www.bellissimapublishing.com

copyright © 2012 by Penny D. Weigand

All rights reserved. No part of this book may be
reproduced or transmitted in any form or by any means,
electronic or mechanical, including photocopying,
recording, or by any other means, or by any information or
storage retrieval system, without permission from the publisher.

ISBN 978-1-61477-026-8
First Edition

All That Glitters Is Not Gold.

A proverb

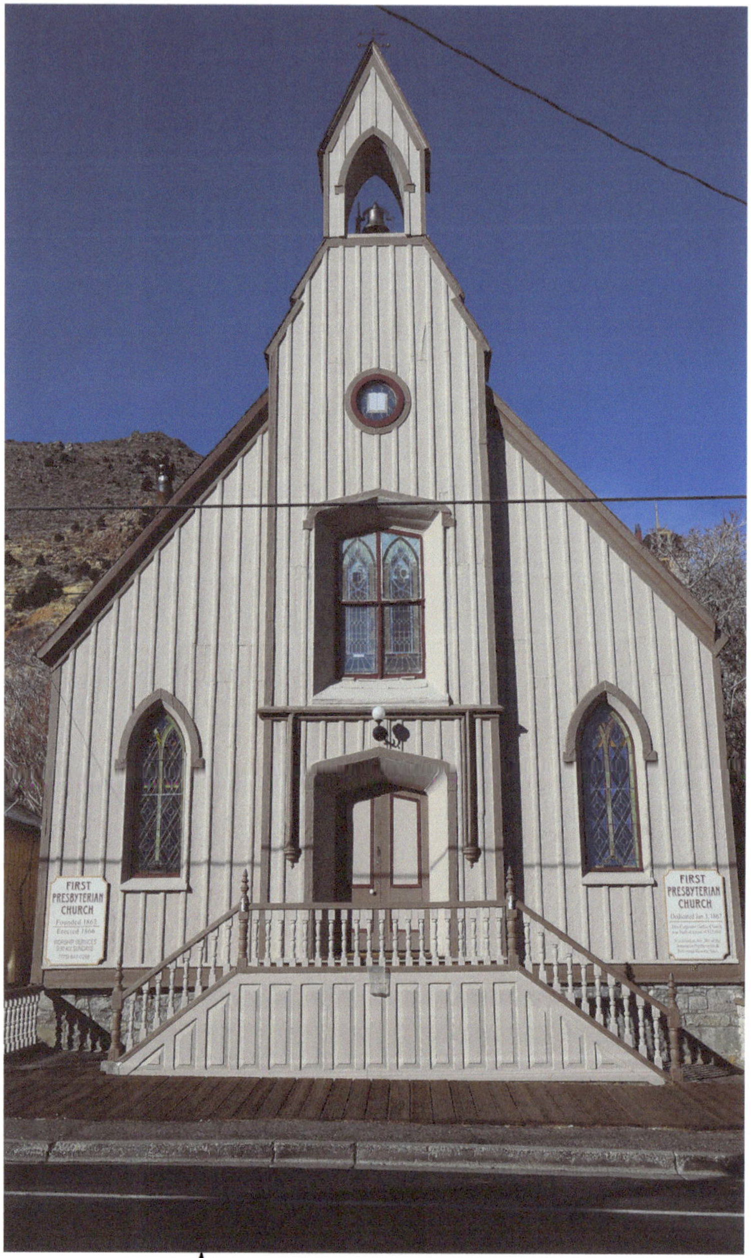

All That Glitters

Bellissima Publishing, LLC

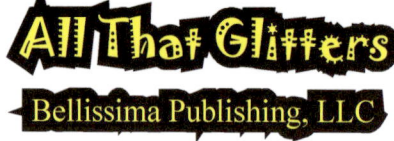

Introduction

Virginia City was a mining boomtown. It appeared virtually overnight as a result of the Comstock Lode silver strike of 1859, found because of the sticky mud washed from the shovels while mining for gold! During its heyday, Virginia City had more than 30,000 residents and was called the richest city in America. Virginia City is also the "birthplace" of Mark Twain, as it was here (in February 1863) that the young writer Samuel Clemens, who was then a reporter for the Territorial Enterprise newspaper, first used his famous pen name, Mark Twain. Virginia City, USA's largest National Historic Landmark, is also listed on the National Register of Historic Places. President Lincoln needed gold and silver to keep the Union solvent during the Civil War, so on October 31, 1864, Lincoln made Nevada a state, even though it didn't have enough people to constitutionally authorize statehood.

Take a trip to this famous city through the lens of John D. Weigand and through the verse of Penelope Dyan, who is an award winning author, attorney and former teacher. Dyan and Weigand see what kids see, and know how to grab their interest. Nothing is spoon fed here as Dyan's intent is to inspire questioning and learning; and this is what she does best, because to learn. . . one begins with inspiration.

All That Glitters
A Kid's Guide To Virginia City, Nevada

Photography By John D. Weigand
Poetry By Penelope Dyan

In historic Virginia you can
step back into time.
And it won't even cost you
a single dime.
Just take your two little feet,
and take a walk
right down the street!

In Virginia City where they found gold and silver ore, you can see a real steam train, (maybe even ride it) and more. And if it is true (as I am told) you can see where they mined all that silver and gold.

Here is the old school house.
(It's not the little red school house of yore.)
There were many classrooms on every floor.

Even today you can stop
at the Virginia City Mercantile
and you can shop!

Mark Twain began writing
in this booming town,
and from this start
became quite renown.
You can visit this museum
and you can see and hear,
just how Mark Twain
began his writing career.
And when you read Tom Sawyer
or Huckleberry Fin,
you can think of this place
where it DID begin!

You can see an 1864 bank vault and tour an underground mine.

You can see a church's steeple,
not far behind.
And as the church bells
ring the hour,
You think of the Comstock Load
and of all of its power.
And you remember the riches
and all the pride,
And how the fame of this place
spread far and wide.

And you can see even MORE!
You can see this firehouse
built in 1864!

And when you take a look inside,
you can see the fire engines
on which the firemen did ride.
More than once
the fire alarms did sound
when Virginia City
burned right to the ground.

But they kept on rebuilding
I am told,
because of the gold and silver
of the Comstock Load.
And here is something
else you can do.
You can pan for gold
right here too!

And as you look at the old clock on the street,
your heart suddenly skips. . .
quite out of beat.

You see a caboose painted red,
and your mom says,
"Now, don't get any ideas
in your little head."
You dream of those times
now long past.
Your mom reminds you,"Things
preserved through time last."
And even though
on this caboose you can't ride,
you can buy a ticket
to ride the steam train inside!

*The greatest wealth
is to live content with little.*

PLATO

www.ingramcontent.com/pod-product-compliance
Ingram Content Group UK Ltd.
Pitfield, Milton Keynes, MK11 3LW, UK
UKHW060132240426
12048UKWH00002B/8